GROW
THROUGH
IT

*How My Struggles with Endometriosis, Infertility, and
Depression Motivated Me to Reclaim My Power!*

By
TAFIEA STOKES

This book is a memoir. It reflects the author's present recollections of experiences over time. Some names and characteristics have been changed, some events have been compressed, and some dialogues have been recreated.

Publisher: Tafiea Stokes
Publisher email: Tafiea.stokes@gmail.com
Publisher website: Tafieastokes.com
ISBN: 978-1-7341390-0-6
Printed in the United States of America
Interior design: Sarco Press
Cover design: Hubspot Pro

Dedication

THIS BOOK IS dedicated to my husband, Jesse. Finding you in this life was one of the most preeminent things that ever happened to me. Before you, I doubted anyone could love me the way you do. Your love is unconditional and selfless. Marrying you was the best decision I have ever made.

As we continue to grow together, I feel your love for me grow more each day. I thank you, from the bottom of my heart, for remaining by my side throughout EVERYTHING.

You are always there to hold my hand and dry my tears, and I can't express how much that touches my heart and soul. You never abandoned me, regardless of my battles. Your love and selflessness have propelled me to flourish into a better woman, not only in the world, but for you as well.

There isn't a damn thing I wouldn't do for you in this life. You are a huge piece of my universe and heart. Thank you so much for being a home for me, supporting me and rooting me on. I love you to the moon and back and can't wait to continue our journey together.

With all my love,

Your wife

Contents

Preface

IN THE MIDST of my battle with endometriosis and infertility, I felt so alone, helpless, and hopeless. Although some family and friends were there for support, they only understood to a certain extent.

I didn't know anyone who walked my path. I had not heard anyone like me speak their truth. I wanted to change that and allow my story to be one that others could relate to, reflect on, and take good from.

Endometriosis, infertility, and depression are more common than anyone speaks of. The conversation is silent due to feelings of shame, embarrassment, or fear. These topics are taboo, and it is time for the stigma to cease. I want to be the voice that starts an echo of other women gaining the confidence and courage to tell their stories, speak up and speak out.

I was tired of living in the shadows under a dark cloud on mute. I had something to say and, in my heart, I knew I needed to. Sharing my story was part of my healing process, getting it all out of my head and onto paper. I am confident it will help women just like me who feel how I felt: alone, helpless, and hopeless.

Before writing this book, I started the Team Syracuse Chapter of Worldwide EndoMarch where I serve as Chapter President. A community of women was formed, all who have similar stories like my own. In addition to supporting one another, we raise awareness through events and fundraisers while continuing to inform the community of the 200 million women affected. 200 million women with minimal treatment options and yet still no cure in sight. Starting this group put me in a position to begin the conversation, gain a voice, and use it to help tell the stories of those 200 million women.

Since starting Team Syracuse Worldwide Endo-March, I have had many women, who either suffer from endometriosis or have similar symptoms of the condition, reach out to me. They heard of the group through word of mouth or saw me on the local news discussing endometriosis. My passion for my activist work was what initially got their attention. Being relatable to their situation was something they desired and appreciated.

I would have never thought I would be someone brave enough to tell my story and use my voice. I know now it is so important to take the time to do so because you never know who is watching, listening, and following. You never know who needs to hear that there's someone just like them walking their same path.

Grow Through It takes you on my journey with the struggles of endometriosis, infertility, and depression. It shines some light on how I was able to weather the storm and keep moving forward, regardless of the dark cloud that tried to follow. A knockdown here, a fall there, but in the end, I still overcame, and from that, I gained strength.

Grow Through It shows you how a woman's life can be impacted by endometriosis and how the effects of this condition trickle-down causing many other health issues to arise. Endometriosis is the gift that keeps on giving while trying to take away!

I've learned that in all aspects of life, you have to keep going, regardless of what gets in the way. While I wrote this, I was hesitant. I did not know if my story would be offensive, too intense, or if I was revealing too much. I came to realize that this is MY STORY and how I tell it expresses who I am and, therefore, is a part of MY STORY. It may not be for everyone, but those who it is for will appreciate the fact I told it. You can't allow the opinions of what people think or may think, stray you in a way to hide your story from the world. It is your story that could make THE DIFFERENCE!

After writing this, I felt countless emotions. I felt

accomplished I had set a goal and completed it. I felt relieved I had started to heal from my struggles. I felt free because I was brave enough to tell my story and didn't let the negative thoughts or opinions impact my decision. I felt proud my story would now be in the hands of many other women just like me with the hopes of empowering them. *Grow Through It* is a long time coming. I hope my story will be of benefit to you or someone you know.

Introduction

ROM STRUGGLE COMES strength, and I hope this is true for you on your journey. I encourage you to read my story and challenge you to begin to develop your own guidance to conquer your battles.

From *Grow Through It,* I believe you will take away a few meaningful points on how to advocate for yourself and grow through your struggles.

Everyone sees a healthcare provider at some point. Are you making the best out of your appointment, getting the most from your time with your provider and understanding what was said at the appointment? This book highlights some of the aspects I believe will help you with these points and help arm you with info so you are better equipped to get the most from the time with your provider, better understand your health situation(s), and advocate for yourself.

Growing through your struggles is the apex of *Grow Through It.* It's so easy to go through a battle and let it dictate your life, what you do, and who you are. That storm gives you a chance to learn from the dark moment and see it for what it is: a dark moment. It is not meant for you to stay in that moment, but to grow and learn from it. It took me a while, but I was able to overcome those hindrances that almost knocked me flat on my face. It's in those dark moments that you are planted!

Read on as we explore the struggles I faced and what I did to help me surpass.

"Your current situation is not your final destination" ~Unknown.

CHAPTER 1

Welcome to Womanhood

I N THE NURSE'S office, every month from the start of my menses, age fourteen, until about age sixteen to seventeen. That is what I remember about how this whole story begins. The nurse's office became my second home during that "time of the month," *e v e r y m o n t h*. I felt I was in there more than I was in class. Every damn time, "Excuse me, can I get a pass to the nurse's office?" I am surprised the teachers in my class didn't already have my pass written out and ready for me each month.

This was a regular occurrence both I and the nurses became accustomed to. Once I arrived at the office, the nurse would contact my mother to pick me up from school due to the excessive pain I'd be in. I am sure the students thought I had some type of disease due to me having to leave class so frequently and always being in the nurse's office. Well, I guess I did have a disease or a condition nonetheless, but one I was not aware of yet.

At age fourteen, I met Aunt Flo for the first time, or as my mother would call it, "Mother Nature." I remember her telling my father about it saying, "Well, Mother Nature knocked on the door for Taf this morning." I shuttered in embarrassment thinking, *Now, why would you go on to tell Dad?*

Anyways, getting my menstrual cycle was not what I envisioned. No, I was not running through dandelion and sunflower gardens while wearing a white flowy dress that blew in the wind as I jumped up in the air in awe of all the natural beauty. I am jealous of the women who could pull that off, but that was not me. During that "time of the month," I was not able to do much at all. I was not running through any gardens, let alone running at all for that matter. I was not able to participate in much physical activity and gym class was off the table. My experience was quite the opposite of what commercials depicted.

I remember that first period; I woke up and went to the bathroom, I had no idea what the hell was going on, and then I realized I had started my period. I was clueless about what to do next. I had seen commercials and heard about "the period," but I needed my mother. I walked into her room. "Mom," I said with a nervous voice, "um, I think *IT* happened." I was hoping my mother would pick up on what "*IT*" was because at age fourteen I was too embarrassed to even say the word "period." That word seemed so taboo to me. Thank God my mother knew what the hell I was talking about. She did not miss a beat.

She sat up in bed and grabbed the phone to call my school and explained to them why I would not be in. I listened to the conversation and felt horrified as my mother spoke. "Yes, Mother Nature knocked on the door this morning for Tafiea, so she will not be attending class today." My mother called out of work and we spent that whole day together. She made herself available for me to ask any questions I needed and she answered all of them without hesitation.

That morning, we went to the store to look at the different sanitary napkins and she explained the numbers, sizes, and when they would be best used. Thank goodness nobody was in those aisles at that time to observe what was taking place. I did not know there were so many different options. You had to choose between brands, sizes, wings or no wings, regular, super, super plus, overnight, scented or unscented, and amount per pack just to name a few options. I mean, this was like some next level shit just for a period. *Who would have thought?* "How do you even choose with all these options?" I asked my mother because, by this point, I was too overwhelmed to even make sense of it all. Again, my mother broke it all down for me in a way that was easy to understand. I must give her props for being such a good mother during that phase in my life and being there with me and for me at that moment.

So, what I got out of that lesson from my mother was that in order to go throughout the day and still function while bleeding daily for three to seven days, I had to put a huge "diaper-type" product between my legs that stuck to my panties all day. I would change the "diaper" throughout the day, but I would need to wear one all day and into the night. Now, during the day, I wore whatever my flow was: light, regular, super, or super plus. At night, I would have another bag of pads for overnight use. The overnight-use pads were the size of a crib-sized mattress and were the most uncomfortable thing to have on while sleeping. That about sums up my takeaway message from that day with my mom.

Women are the most glamorous species on earth and yet we must wear the least alluring things once a month. Like no one has figured this shit out yet? All the technology in the world and women are left with bullshit options during our monthly bleed, what the hell? Oh, let's not forget about when I had to go out in public with these bulky "diapers" on between my legs. On top of the situation already being chaotic, I also had to make sure no one would be able to tell I had on a pad by wearing pants that were not too tight to reveal the big pad bulge. Sounds wonderful, right? Wrong, so damn wrong!

Being uncomfortable while bleeding on a pad that

collected between my legs, being self-conscious about what to wear, and making sure not to wear white or a skirt or a dress around the time my period was due, at age fourteen, was more than enough work for me. Talk about creating anxiety at a young age. Oh, and tampons were even less intriguing to me at that age. I was not too fond of sticking a foreign object up my vagina every few hours, then removing it full of blood. No, thank you! Being a woman was giving me a headache already and I was just starting out!

Around my second period, I began to experience this extreme cramping that would literally bring me to my knees. I thought to myself, *Well, now, this just can't be right.* I am in no way or form exaggerating the extreme part of this at all. I never knew cramps would be so debilitating. Again, I reverted to the appealing commercials of those lovely girls and women with their beautiful makeup placed perfectly on their faces, white pants while playing some very physical sports, and wearing a huge smile. What a bullshit representation of what really goes on; well, for me, anyway. Where were the commercials that portrayed the real deal? I wanted to see commercials portraying how it sucked to bleed for three to seven days monthly for the majority of your existence. Where were the commercials where women like me were sitting on the couch or lying in bed with a heating pad, drinking herbal tea and continuing to be in excruciating pain for days? Like, come on, portray the spectrum of everything that could happen, **ALL** the possibilities!

The cramps that I experienced felt as if someone was stabbing me on the inside from many different angles and reopening cuts repeatedly making the bleeding last longer and become heavier. Sounds bad, right? Imagine how that feels! I often thought to myself, *If this is womanhood, then I would rather be a Toys R Us kid.* Seriously, this was not how I wanted to take on adulthood. Who thought that it was a good idea to create women to bleed on a monthly basis? I would need to curl up in the fetal position to ease some of the pain. My two new best friends, the heating pad and herbal tea, were always there when I needed them. The warmth from the tea and the temperature from the heating pad would take a little of the edge off. The heating pad warming from the outside and the tea from the inside. It made the pain more tolerable to where I could do things, you know like roll to the other side, sit up, or breath regularly. No, I am being dead serious.

The worst part was when I got into a comfortable position, then my bladder decided it needed to be emptied. I would never be able to find the right angle of that position again if I moved. The struggle was seriously real. I could not imagine going through this every month for the rest of my life. On top of that, the average woman has 450 plus periods in her lifetime! **450 PERIODS!!!!** What crap!

At that time, not knowing any better, my hope was that I would get used to this monthly monster and learn to deal and cope with the pain, length, and flow of my period. I figured since I was just starting out, my body needed time to adjust to the change and things would get better for me with time. I did not think this was something I would need to seek medical care for later. I thought this was life and I had to suck it up and literally put my big girl panties on and handle it. I was doing everything I knew how to do, using the heating pad, drinking herbal tea, resting, and taking it easy during these temporary times of unbearable pain, which, for me, began to last a full seven days.

However, even these remedies did not relieve the pain and only gave very short-term relief. As for the length and flow, I had no remedy. I tried the over-the-counter menstrual cramp pain relievers with the pretty packaging but to no avail. This evil song and dance went on to last for two to three years before I would be encouraged to seek medical advice. Two to three years of missed school for a few days per month. Two to three years of dealing with unbearable pain. Two to three years of missing family events. Two to three years of lying in bed for about a week per month. Two to three years of pure torture, hell, and despair. Two to three years of missing out on my life because of THE MONTHLY MONSTER!

CHAPTER 2
Birth Control Roulette

I WAS IN CLASS and, of course, the monthly monster decided to surprise me. I went to the nurse's office, as was my norm, and this time the nurse said to me, "Honey, have you been to your doctor to talk about the pain you have every time you have your period?"

I replied, "No, I thought this was something normal that girls and women went through."

She went on to say, "I really think you should speak to your parents and have them take you to your doctor to find out if anything else is going on. The pain you have monthly is not normal."

I replied, "Thank you, and I definitely will speak to them to get an appointment scheduled with my doctor."

Age seventeen is when my school nurse insisted my pain was NOT NORMAL. She suggested I seek medical care to investigate if there was an underlying issue and/or treatment for my symptoms. Seeking medical advice had come to mind, but I thought the pain was normal and my body was not used to it yet. By the worry and concern in the school nurse's voice, I knew this was not the case. I had never had anyone else insist that the pain was not normal. My family never really seemed too concerned, and my teachers never said anything. Thank goodness for my school nurse recognizing that my symptoms were NOT NORMAL.

I took the advice of my school nurse. I explained to my mother what she said, and Mom quickly made an appointment.

When the doctor entered the room, I explained what had been going on for the last two to three years… The times I went to the nurse's office and was sent home because I was not able to concentrate on classes or sit comfortably due to pain. How I would lie at home waiting for the pain to stop, using heating pads and drinking herbal tea for seven days. How it was hard for me to get in a comfortable position. How over-the-counter medications did nothing for relief. After explaining everything to my doctor, she diagnosed me with dysmenorrhea.

Dysmenorrhea means painful periods.

She thought the best solution to help decrease my pain and the length of the period was birth control methods. After she had a conversation with my mother and me, we agreed on Depo-Provera. This was a birth control method with a common side effect of weight gain, and since I was underweight, my mother figured it could also help with this factor. Depo-Provera was convenient and was something I would not have to remember to take every day, as it was administered every three months.

I gave Depo-Provera a try, and for three months straight, I bled. I thought to myself, *There is no damn way that I am going to stay on a medication that causes me to bleed even more than I am already bleeding.* I refused to suffer even more than I was suffering. I was seventeen for heaven's sake. This was not cute! I went to my doctor and expressed my frustration. I explained this method was not user-friendly and was causing more harm. Her advice was to wait it out. She thought if I gave Depo-Provera a little more time, I would begin to reap the benefits of its use. I did not quite understand it, but she was the professional and I trusted her.

I stayed on this medication for nine more months and noticed a slight decrease in pain and the periods ended up stopping. However, this decrease in symptoms was only temporarily. (SIDE NOTE: It did not help me gain weight as my mother had hoped.) With use for nine months, I had daily spotting and I began to have mood swings. I would cry at the drop of a dime for situations that did not warrant a need to shed tears. I could be sad, and then I was fine; then I was mad, but stayed quiet; then I was depressed. I was on a literal emotional rollercoaster. I could not continue to deal with all the side effects. My mother, doctor, and I agreed I should not continue to take Depo-Provera. There were multiple birth control methods and brands tried after this and none have helped with all of the symptoms.

Birth control roulette, a lovely game I am still playing as I sit here and write this.

CHAPTER 3
Welcome to Adulthood

I WAS NOW TWENTY-TWO years old, five years since being diagnosed with dysmenorrhea. NSAIDs, over-the-counter analgesics, heat and birth control methods, and nothing was completely taking the pain away. The most the birth control did was decrease bleeding and length of my period. Five years later, and no progression in getting to a pain-free state.

The pain became so unbearable; it began to impact my job and social life more than before. I just started a new job, my first job as an RN. Because of my periods, I would call in every few months due to the severity of cramps. The pain was on a monthly basis, but at times I was able to tolerate it and still function to some degree. As far as out-of-office social activities went, I had to be mindful the event was not around the time of my period. Just like five years ago, I was absent from many family activities as well. Because of the hold "killer cramps" had on me, I sought further help.

I started with my primary care provider who was a different doctor than previously. I explained my symptoms, and how my social life and job were impacted. She explained that based on my symptoms and explanation, it sounded as if I had what is known as endometriosis.

Endometriosis is a painful disorder in which endometrial-like tissue (tissue that resembles the lining that normally covers the inside of the uterus) grows outside of the uterus on organs. The endometrial growths bleed monthly mimicking the menses. Besides pain, it can cause gastrointestinal issues, and binding of your organs as well as many other varying symptoms.

The only way to diagnose endometriosis was via surgery. This was not a step she wanted to take until I was at the stage in life where I was ready to have children. In the case it was endometriosis, she would be able to remove the lesions and make it easier for me to be able to conceive, as endometriosis can impact fertility. In the interim, I would have to continue with taking birth control to help decrease some of the symptoms. She suggested I try NuvaRing. This was one birth control method I had not attempted and I was open-minded, as nothing in the past had worked fully.

After a while of using the NuvaRing, I did notice a decrease in pain, length, and flow of my menstrual cycle. I hoped this method would continue to help keep the pain manageable.

After a few months, my doctor noticed that my blood pressure spiked. She agreed to let me continue to use NuvaRing, but I would also need to take another medication to lower my blood pressure. Twenty-two with high blood pressure and a plethora of other symptoms. Great way to start adulthood. All I was missing was my AARP card.

CHAPTER 4

Now This Shit...Literally

A S TIME PASSED, gastrointestinal symptoms such as alternating constipation and diarrhea as well as bloating, food aversions, and nausea started to make an appearance with my period. *Oh shit, for real? Now this?* I made an appointment to see my primary care provider. She referred me to a gastroenterologist to be evaluated further, who wasted no time getting to the bottom of the issue. Before my initial appointment with the gastroenterologist, I had to complete an upper GI series.

Upper GI series is an x-ray exam of your upper GI tract that is made visible by drinking a liquid solution / contrast.

This was *the l o n g e s t* appointment I had ever been to. Thank goodness I did not have to wait alone as my now-husband, Jesse, came with me for moral support. When we arrived, I was directed to change into a gown and given a foam cup filled with a thick, white liquid.

I was sure drinking the white liquid would make all those gastrointestinal symptoms worst just by the look of it. It tasted like watered-down chalk, but I tried to ignore the taste and finish it as fast as I could. After finishing, I had to have x-rays taken every few mins until the contrast was cleared out of my system. We were there for about two to three hours as this appointment dragged on. After the test, I was instructed to schedule an actual appointment to see the provider and discuss the results and next steps.

I returned to the office about a week later. It was not long before my name was called, and I was taken into an exam room. The doctor entered immediately. He introduced himself, explained the results of the imaging I completed a week prior and started to explain what he believed the diagnosis was. Based on my presentation and symptoms, and normal upper GI series, he believed I had irritable bowel syndrome.

Irritable bowel syndrome is an intestinal disorder causing symptoms such as abdominal pain, nausea, vomiting, diarrhea, and constipation.

There was a medication he recommended I try to help relieve some of the gastrointestinal symptoms: amitriptyline, a tricyclic antidepressant, which, prescribed at lower doses, also relieves symptoms associated with irritable bowel syndrome. At that point, I figured trying something that could help relieve the abdominal pain, change in bowel habits, nausea, and vomiting would not hurt as much as the pain as I was already dealing with. I agreed to try the medication. *Yay, another medication to add to my home pharmacy. Should have purchased stock with the pharmacy.*

After a few weeks, I realized some of the symptoms, such as abdominal pain and bloating, decreased, my bowel habits were normalizing, and nausea lessened. With symptoms dwindling, I was so hopeful and relieved and continued with this regimen for quite a while.

CHAPTER 5

Standing Tall

SYMPTOMS CONTINUED TO fluctuate and present in different ways. One morning, I woke up ready to go to work and my right lower abdomen was in intense pain. While I was getting ready to head to the car, Jesse noticed that my posture was not normal and I was sort of bent over walking. He asked if I was okay and if I wanted to go to the emergency room instead. I told him I would be fine, and if things worsened, I would call and let him know. We proceeded to the car as he drove me to work. Before I got out of the car, he made sure to ask again if I would be okay and I felt as if I would be fine with time.

I figured the pain was temporary and would go away with time. When I arrived at my unit, my co-workers observed how I was walking. They immediately sent me to the emergency room to be assessed.

I called Jesse and he turned around to come to sit with me while I waited to be evaluated.

I was put in the observation area immediately. The pain in my abdomen was horrible, but I was used to being in some degree of pain, so I was not fazed. The nurse placed an IV in my arm, administered morphine, and gave me a warm cup of what looked like watered-down Kool-Aid. I needed to drink the full cup in order to have a CT scan to evaluate my abdomen. When given the morphine, I had a reaction that caused my body to tense up and I had difficulty swallowing. I was in the right place for an emergency.

After the side effect dissipated, I was able to drink the watered-down Kool-Aid, which tasted even worse than it looked. Some ice cubes would have made it more delectable and helped it to go down smoother. Shortly after finishing the drink, my bed was wheeled into the room where the CT scan would take place. The radiologist helped me on the cold hard table and my body was then covered with a machine that made me feel enclosed and nervous. I was told to hold my breath on certain parts and breathe normally on others as the radiologist took pictures of my abdomen. The scan did not last long, and before I knew it, I was wheeled back into my room. I now had to wait for the doctor to come in, review my results, and explain what was next.

When he finally came into the room, he told me

the imaging was normal and I would be discharged home with ibuprofen for pain relief. He thought the pain was related to dysmenorrhea. This could have been the case, but up until then, I had never had pain which affected my posture. *If the imaging was fine, maybe today was just a fluke.* I took the doctor's advice, took my prescription, and headed home. I was so relieved to be going home to relax in hopes the pain would cease. Maybe some relaxation was all I needed.

That next day, I was off from work and had additional time to relax. The pain decreased and I was starting to stand tall and walk normal again. *Okay, weird, but the doctor was right.*

CHAPTER 6
After All That...Back to Square One

NOT LONG AFTER that first emergency room visit, I would need to visit again. I was going to classes and not able to stand up straight, once again. I was not about to miss any classes or assignments, so I tolerated the pain as I normally did. At the end of the evening, my friend advised me to go to the doctor to be evaluated. It had been a few uncomfortable hours in school for me. Luckily, my provider's office had night hours. I was able to be evaluated that same night.

My mother was kind enough to go with me. When I arrived, the doctor evaluated and palpated my abdomen to further assess. He was convinced I had appendicitis and sent me to the hospital as a direct admission. *Oh great, surgery.* My mother took me to the hospital and helped me get settled in my room before the transporter was there to take me to the operating room. *Ok, this must really be emergent. What the hell did the doctor feel during the exam?* It all went so fast.

When I woke up from surgery I was back in my room with my mom and Jesse. The nurse administered Lortab to help with post-op pain. Shortly after taking the medication, I began to see things crawling all over my body. *What in the entire hell?* I was convinced that there were bugs on my skin, the bed, and the floor. I had to take a shower, change my sheets, and get new hospital socks because the ones I had on were now infested. I used chucks pads on the entire floor to ensure my feet did not touch the bug infestation.

LADIES AND GENTLEMEN... there was no damn bug infestation! Talk about a bad allergy. According to my mother, both she and my grandmother have similar reactions when they take Lortab. The story is, when anesthesia was wearing off, I apparently told my mom to shut up when she tried to inform the nurse a bad reaction might occur. My mother did just that, she shut up and allowed the nurse to continue to give the Lortab. *What the hell, Mom.* She laughs about it to this day, and as for me, not so much. Again, the perfect place to be for this type of ordeal. I was immediately given Benadryl and shortly after was able to calm down, and the "bugs" disappeared.

Looking back and talking about it, I was damn sure

out of my mind after taking some Lortab. Y'all can add that to my known drug allergies along with the morphine!

The next morning, the surgeon came in and explained my appendix was not inflamed or diseased. However, they did see a cyst on my ovary that had burst. There was quite a bit of residual blood surrounding it. This explained the pain I was experiencing a couple of weeks prior.

So, I just had what I would consider a major surgery to remove an organ that did not require removal. On the flip side, it was a good thing that I had an answer to why this new right quadrant pain was occurring. I had cysts that would grow and intermittently burst.

An ovarian cyst is a solid or fluid filled sac within or on the surface of the ovary.

This put me at some ease knowing there was an answer and that meant doctors would better know how to treat the issue, right?

The next day, I was discharged. Recovery was not as bad as I had anticipated, and I was back to work within a week. I visited my primary care provider for a follow-up, and because of the ovarian cyst that was found in surgery, she recommended that I be further evaluated by a gynecologist.

When I went to see the gynecologist, they informed me that the best treatment for the recurrent ovarian cysts would be to continue with birth control. They suggested changing it to oral contraceptives or "the pill." I was informed the pill would help shrink the cysts better than the use of NuvaRing. *Really, my goodness with the birth control already!* I would take this pill for the next few years until I was ready to conceive. Birth control roulette all over again. I began to feel as if birth control was the answer to everything!

CHAPTER 7

Mission: Baby

JESSE AND I dated for six months before we were engaged, and two years later, we were married. You can say we were 1000 percent in love. We wasted no time, and both knew right away. I knew like immediately; I was just waiting for the ring! Throughout our relationship and about a year into marriage, I continued with "the pill." After a year of being married, Jesse and I felt we were ready to take that next step and begin to try for a baby.

I stopped the birth control and we tried naturally for about a year or so. We tracked my cycle, purchased ovulation kits, and did everything we knew how to in order to improve our chances. During that year, I continued to deal with chronic pain and other symptoms that came along with my period but tried to manage the best I could. There was no one method that worked and I tried a plethora of things to help get through. I forgot how unpleasant my symptoms used to be before I started to play birth control roulette. *Holy shit, what was I doing? This was hell on earth!* I knew, in the end, it would all be worth it, so I persevered.

After a year with no success, I went back to see my gynecologist and informed him that my husband and I had been unsuccessful in conceiving. Multiple ultrasounds and blood tests were ordered to evaluate my fertility. The last ultrasound showed signs of multiple ovarian cysts and I was told I had hydrosalpinx affecting my left fallopian tube.

Hydrosalpinx is a blocked fallopian tube filled with fluid.

The gynecologist advised that I immediately have surgery to remove the affected fallopian tube. He explained that even with one of the tubes removed, I would still be able to conceive with IVF. As I listened to him and tried to digest the information, I pumped the brakes. *Skkrrrrrtttttt.* With something so delicate and so sacred as my reproductive system that would be used to produce a new life in the world, I felt I needed to have a second opinion, and if for some reason I was not satisfied with that, then, hell, I would go for a third opinion as well. The gynecologist provided me with the name of a fertility specialist and I immediately called to make an appointment.

The waiting period for the appointment was a few weeks. I used that time to research everything about hydrosalpinx and endometriosis. I was not quite sure if endometriosis was a factor at that time, but I remembered my primary care provider mentioned it in the past. I wanted to be armed with all the knowledge I needed. Knowledge is power and NOTHING was going to stop me from my goal, MISSION: BABY!

CHAPTER 8

Let's Try a Holistic Approach

I N MY RESEARCH, I discovered there was a test used to confirm the diagnosis of hydrosalpinx, hysterosalpingography or HSG for short.

HSG (hysterosalpingogram) is a test in which a dye is placed through the cervix and x-rays are then taken to evaluate. The test helps to determine if the tubes are blocked as well as help determine the shape of the uterus.

HSG was something I wanted to discuss further, once I was able to see the fertility specialist. In the interim, I continued to research like there was nothing else that mattered in the world, and at that time in my life and in my world, this was the truth. I found numerous holistic and natural remedies backed by studies and I could not wait to try them out.

Castor oil packs were the first thing my husband and I tried. Soaking a cloth in castor oil is said to improve circulation and assist in the healing process of organs and tissues. We would soak a small piece of flannel in castor oil. Then I would lie on my back placing the cloth on my pelvis and then a heating pad on top of the cloth. I would leave this in place for about an hour. I stuck to this regimen a few days per week and once to twice per day. This ritual gave me time to take everything in only focusing on MISSION: BABY.

I discovered that acupuncture was proven to be effective in improving fertility.

Fertility acupuncture is said to help by decreasing stress and increasing blood flow to the reproductive systems. With this process, the endocrine system is also balanced.

Fertility acupuncture was something I wanted to attempt. I believed all the holistic interventions together would increase our chances three-fold and was happy holistic approaches existed as another option. I found the perfect acupuncturist, Annette Burden. I worked with her in the past and forgot she also had her own business. I called and immediately set up a consultation.

When I arrived to see Annette, her room was so comforting and welcoming. She was very thorough in her approach and took a full medical history. She informed me she had experience with acupuncture for fertility, massage, and cupping. She helped other women who dealt with fertility issues by using these techniques. She was well-versed and knowledgeable on the topic, and because of that, I had total faith and was ready to add these techniques to my regimen of holistic approaches.

I began to go to Annette once weekly. Every week, we would alternate treatment between fertility massage, cupping, and fertility acupuncture. Annette was so positive, down-to-earth, nurturing, and caring. Her passion for her clients really showed through her work.

After going to Annette weekly for about a month or so, she suggested an herbal formula. I knew a little about this from my research but had not found anyone who specialized. I agreed to her suggestion and she developed a formula of herbs I would need for treatment based on my medical history and symptoms. About a week or so later, I received the herbs in the mail. The directions read to use one spoonful of the mixture in hot water twice per day. This mixture was very bland, but I did as Annette instructed and used the herb formula every day.

My mood and mental changed for the better as I stuck to my holistic regimen. I felt hopeful and knew in the right circumstances I would be able to conceive. I was in a more positive mind space, and although I was in this situation, I knew I was not alone. The process made me stronger because I had to work twice as hard to get to the goal and I was determined to make it happen by doing whatever it took.

CHAPTER 9
A Breath of Fresh Air

J WAS EAGER TO get to the fertility clinic. My mind was hopeful, open, and full of only positive thoughts. The day finally came to meet Dr. Robert Kiltz. I arrived not knowing what to expect, but my expectations were exceeded. The office was beautiful, peaceful, and home-like. The staff was very friendly and welcoming and helped to put my mind at ease. I thought we would be meeting in an exam room with an exam table and all the nerve-wracking medical equipment. However, Jesse and I met Dr. Kiltz in a room that reminded me of a living room. Comfortable atmosphere, colored walls, three chairs, and a cozy leather couch. This was a good change of scenery.

Dr. Kiltz sat down with us and allowed us to tell our story. After listening, he verbalized his thoughts, suggestions, and concerns. He made sure we understood everything and used diagrams and pictures to help us visualize certain points. I felt we were definitely in good hands.

I asked about the HSG testing during our conversation. He agreed the HSG would be appropriate and necessary. He explained the procedure could cause a little pain and cramping during and shortly after. I had been going through more than enough pain with my periods, and being off of all birth control was a nightmare. I inquired about general anesthesia for the procedure. He understood my concern and was agreeable. Before leaving the office, we scheduled the HSG testing.

After meeting Dr. Kiltz, we quickly learned he was very passionate, caring, down-to-earth and knowledgeable. He was an amazing spirit and his bedside manner was top notch. I put all my trust in him. He made it known that he would do what it took to help us accomplish the goal of MISSION: BABY.

The day arrived for the HSG, and Jesse and I arrived before the roosters were out. The procedure was performed right in the comfort of the office, on the opposite side of the building from the consultation room we were in weeks prior. We sat in the waiting room for a short period before being called in the back. I was taken to what appeared to be an OR room and was given a gown to change in to. I settled in, and shortly after, Dr. Kiltz walked in and explained all we needed to know about the procedure and what I could expect after. The anesthesiologist walked in next, introduced himself, what he would be giving, and then prepped and began to administer the medications. I remember seeing his face and then only remember waking up next to my nurse and husband.

Dr. Kiltz walked in as I was waking up and informed us that based on the HSG, my fallopian tubes were not blocked. *What a relief.* Both tubes were fine. *Wow, I could have totally gone the wrong way and got surgery to remove the tube prior to getting further evaluation.* Thank goodness that hydrosalpinx was not the situation that we were dealing with. I spent all that time beating myself up thinking the tube was blocked and I would have to go through more extreme measures to resolve the issue. I was overwhelmed with emotion because my worst fear had been proven false. *Thank you, thank you, thank you!*

Dr. Kiltz suggested Jesse have a sperm analysis to find out if this played a factor in our inability to conceive. The next week, we went back to the office with a sample in hand. It was not long before we received a call saying Jesse's sperm was fine with no abnormalities. So now that he was ruled out as the issue, we focused on finding out why my body would not cooperate with our attempts.

After Jesse was cleared, Dr. Kiltz mentioned the next course of action would be to have exploratory laparoscopic surgery to determine if endometriosis was the cause of infertility and if so, he would remove the endometrial growths to help give us a better chance to conceive.

Exploratory laparoscopic surgery is a minimally invasive surgery in which the surgeon places tiny incisions in your abdominal wall to look at the abdominal and reproductive organs to help diagnose certain diseases.

Both Jesse and I agreed we wanted to proceed with surgery. We scheduled surgery and had to wait two months before we would have an answer.

As we waited, I went on to continue with my natural, holistic remedies, including my regimen of herbal supplements twice daily, acupuncture/massage/cupping weekly, and castor oil packs. The spa that was connected to the fertility clinic offered fertility yoga. I signed up for classes and added this to my regimen, once weekly. Although we now knew the tubes were not blocked, we also knew that endometriosis was a possible factor and that many of the interventions were beneficial for that as well as overall infertility, regardless of what the cause was.

CHAPTER 10

Finally, an Answer

LL THOSE YEARS ago, my primary care provider mentioned endometriosis and thought this was a condition I could have. So here it was, the time I was ready to conceive, and I would finally get an answer about my inability to conceive, but also the question I had been wondering about for years, if I had endometriosis. This was a long time coming and I was ready for some type of an answer. It's not that I wanted an endometriosis diagnosis, but I was tired of not knowing what the hell was wrong with my body and then having to play the waiting game for years. Those couple of months flew by, and before we knew it, the day for surgery was staring us in the face.

We had to wake up at the crack of dawn, September 11, 2014; Jesse, my mother, and I proceeded to the outpatient center for the surgery. I was the only patient in the office lobby at this time and we were not there long before my name was called to get prepped and ready for what was to come. The rooms were very tiny. It was not much of a room at all. This was the location where the preops were placed prior to going directly to the OR. I was the first patient that morning for surgery and was told I would not have to wait long. Knowing I was first to have surgery did not scare me as much as the thought of the damn IV. I literally asked for EMLA for my hand to numb the area.

EMLA is an anesthetic that is used to numb the skin prior to a medical procedure.

I had so much trust in this doctor, but the IV, forget it, especially in my hand. I can only imagine what the nurse thought at that time. Here I am, a grown-ass woman asking for some damn EMLA for an IV placement. Oh well, what can I say?

I had not waited long at all before the anesthesiologist arrived to introduce himself and then Dr. Kiltz came in to see me and explained the surgery again. He looked around at Jesse and my mother as he spoke making sure neither of them nor I had any questions before proceeding. All of our questions were answered, and we were just ready to go ahead and get some answers. The nurse raised my bed and wheeled me out in the direction of the OR. I remember the anesthesia being started on the way to the OR and don't remember anything after.

When I woke up, Jesse, my aunt, my mother,

and my brother were in recovery with me. I was still groggy, but remember seeing imaging on a screen to the right of me, what I later knew as being my reproductive and abdominal organs. The image looked like a thousand spider webs entangled with one another with short, thicker, and thinner areas connected with a thick sticky-like substance. I couldn't believe this was what was going on inside of me. *What the hell? What did this mean? Why did it look like that?* Without waiting long to find out the answers, Dr. Kiltz came in to speak to me and my family. He went on to say I did indeed have endometriosis, stage 4. The endometriosis was on my fallopian tubes, ovaries, and bowels.

Stage 4 endometriosis is the "severe" stage where deep endometriosis implants, cysts, and adhesions invade your organs.

An adhesion is scar tissue that binds together and acts as a binding agent, causing organs to stick together. Adhesions normally form after surgery.

He removed as much as the endometriosis as he could and, in addition to the exploratory surgery, he completed lysis of adhesions.

The lysis of adhesions is a procedure in which scar tissue that causes chronic pelvic and abdominal pain is destroyed.

He felt my chances of conceiving had improved after surgery. I was very confident, and I was very hopeful that we would now be able to conceive.

We discussed what the next move would be once I was recovered. Dr. Kiltz thought it would be beneficial to try IUI. We were agreeable and ready to get the process started.

IUI is intrauterine insemination in which the sperm is placed in the uterus to facilitate fertilization.

CHAPTER 11

Emotional Rollercoaster

ABOUT A MONTH after surgery, we scheduled our first IUI. Everything was moving so smoothly with Dr. Kiltz. We were so excited to have an answer and now, hopefully, a solution. The spa that the fertility clinic was connected to offered acupuncture. This was a great addition to the clinic because it gave those who used fertility acupuncture a chance to continue with their regimen. Feeling the benefits of acupuncture with Annette, I decided to continue with acupuncture before fertility treatments.

December 1, 2014; the morning of the IUI procedure, Jesse had to provide a semen sample for the procedure. Prior to the IUI procedure, we walked to the back of the building, which was just as equally welcoming and serene as the fertility center office. I was given a robe at the front desk after checking in, and Jesse and I proceeded upstairs to where acupuncture would take place. The waiting room was a huge, cozy room with leather recliners, dimmed lights, and a beautiful fireplace. Shortly after sitting down, a guy came to the room and called us to the back.

I was instructed to get relaxed and he would be back in to start the treatment. I hopped on the table, under the sheet and in a deep state of relaxation as we waited for the acupuncturist to return. A few needles were placed between my eyebrows, one on my forehead and a few on my abdomen, and a heating lamp moved over my abdomen. He informed me to continue to relax and he would return in a few moments. I sat there with Jesse, quiet, relaxing, and thinking positive thoughts and how that bundle of joy would feel to finally have in my stomach. I envisioned my baby moving inside of me for the first time and tried to imagine how that would feel.

Not sure how much time had passed, but before I knew it, the acupuncturist was back to remove the heat lamp and needles. A few moments later, Dr. Kiltz entered the room smiling, so warm and positive, and his aura entered before he did. I do not remember much of this first IUI besides the fact that the doctor said, "We are going to get you that baby." In my heart and from his passion, I knew he would indeed help us to conceive our child finally.

I had to return to work after this procedure as did my husband. At work, I was giddy and nervous thinking about all the possibilities and my new bundle of joy. My adrenaline was very high and I had a hard time focusing on anything else.

A couple of days had passed, and I had to return to the fertility center to get lab work completed to check hCG levels to see if the IUI worked.

hCG (human chorionic gonadotropin) is a hormone that is produced during pregnancy after implantation takes place.

Another early morning appointment, but I did not care how early I had to get up as long as we were getting closer to the goal. I arrived and did not wait long that morning before I was called in the back for my lab work.

Again, I headed right to work from this appointment. By afternoon, I could not wait anymore and decided to call and ask about results. I was so nervous and scared about what the outcome was, but I was so hopeful it worked. I waited to hear the voice on the other end of the line, and she informed me that the IUI cycle had not worked this time. I was a little sad, but still hopeful as this was the beginning of our journey and I knew it could take a few tries before we got the result we wanted.

I completed the rest of my day at work and then went home and researched how to improve the chances of IUI, what medication combinations would work best, herbal remedies, and holistic approaches to

IUI. I was still MISSION: BABY and I needed more ammo. Jesse finally arrived home and I informed him of the outcome, and we agreed we would try again.

That next morning, we called to schedule another IUI treatment. This time, I wanted to try something different that I had read in my research that could improve the chances of IUI. I expressed this to Dr. Kiltz when I saw him for the prep for the next round of IUI. To my surprise, Dr. Kiltz was open to my suggestion and willing to give it a go, to see if it would help.

My research led me to an article that suggested that having an IUI on two consecutive days and having acupuncture both before and after the procedures increased the chances. I took two consecutive days off work so I would be able to go home and rest after the procedures. Jesse was not able to make these two appointments due to work issues. Although I had to go by myself, I stayed in contact with my loving husband throughout and continued to have a positive mindset.

December 29, 2014; I went to the fertility clinic early in the morning and went over to the spa to have acupuncture prior to IUI. It was the same routine as my prior IUI. The acupuncturist placed a couple of needles in my forehead and abdomen, and the heat lamp over my abdomen. This seemed to last a little longer than the first time, but before I knew it, the acupuncturist was back in removing the needles.

A few minutes later, Dr. Kiltz entered with test

tubes, a catheter and other supplies that were needed for the procedure. This procedure was quick and felt as if it only took a few minutes before Dr. Kiltz was leaving the room and the acupuncturist reentering the room again placing a few needles in my forehead and my abdomen, and the heat lamp over my abdomen. I took a deep breath and tried my best to relax and hoped that something was going on in there. *Come on fertilization, give us a baby*. Shortly after, the acupuncturist walked back in to remove the heat lamp and acupuncture needles, and I was sent on my way.

After IUI day number one, I went home to lie down and relax. I watched *Lifetime* for the rest of the evening trying to remain positive and optimistic. Now that I think of it, I probably should have chosen something other than *Lifetime* to keep my mind busy and stress-free.

Day two for IUI, and again, I had to wake up at the ass crack of dawn. I had the same acupuncturist and the same room from IUI day one. Again, we went through the same steps as IUI day number one. After all was done I went home to lay down and rest. I took a good nap which is just what I needed after all the back and forth to the fertility clinic and rollercoaster of emotions I was feeling.

Days later, I had to go get lab work done again to check my hCG levels to determine if the IUIs worked. I was so hopeful at this point. *Oh yea, I know that you worked this time, come on, baby.* When I got the call in the afternoon, I felt so "fuzzy" with excitement. However, I was told by the voice on the other end of the phone that again the IUIs did not take. My heart sunk, my body felt tingling, and I became so mad, sad and angry all in one. I felt disappointed in myself. It was my fault in the first place that I could not give my husband a child naturally. Now even with the use of science, I was still failing as a woman. *What is wrong with you?* I was so hard on myself about this. Failure did not fit me well and that is all I felt was failure! Who would want to stay with someone who was not able to provide them with a family? I felt so lost, hopeless, and helpless.

Days later, I went back to the fertility center to discuss the IUIs and other options. Dr. Kiltz suggested that after having tried three IUIs, IVF would be the next step.

IVF (in vitro fertilization) is a combination of medications and medical procedures which helps the sperm to fertilize an egg. The eggs are retrieved from the woman after helping to get to an optimal state. Once they are retrieved, the egg(s) and sperm are manually combined in a dish. Once fertilization takes place, then the egg(s) are placed back in the uterus.

He suggested I maintain a low-carb, no-sugar diet, as this would make the endometriosis worse, which in turn would worsen the issues with infertility. He informed me that the longer I waited to start IVF, the more the chances would decrease because the endometriosis would grow back.

At that point, I just needed an emotional break. The emotional rollercoaster of hoping, wishing, waiting, and getting test results had begun to take a toll on me and my mind. In addition to this, I was still struggling with painful periods, which we now knew was from the endometriosis.

CHAPTER 12

Coming Out of the Dark, Into the Light

I FELT SO DEFEATED, depressed, hopeless, and helpless. I felt less than a woman. I never knew anyone in my family or otherwise that struggled with the issues of conceiving. What had I done to piss off the Baby Gods to take me through all of this? My mood was lowered; I was tearful when thinking of not being able to have a baby. I thought about what would happen if I wasn't able to. A baby is something that I wanted forever. I know that this was something that my husband wanted for a long time as well. I did not want to disappoint my husband. I wouldn't want him to stay with me if I couldn't give him his dream family.

All these thoughts were going through my head. I started to have a decrease in appetite, and I did not want to get out of bed. All I wanted to do was sleep. I was helpless and I was going further and further down the black hole. I was aware of this and I knew I needed to do something to lift myself up out of the dirt.

Soon after having these thoughts, one day, on my lunch break, I went to my stepmother's home. I told her what was going on and how I felt. I had never really opened up to her about anything emotional in the past, but there was a strong urge to go to her about how I was feeling. Thank goodness I have such an awesome stepmother that took time out of her day to listen and talk me through those feelings. She was very encouraging and inspirational. She told me everything would work out and it would happen when it happened and when it is meant to happen. She recommended I read a book she had read in the past when she was in a rough spot and it changed her life.

At first, I was skeptical about the book. *At this point, there was no way a book was going to change my life. I had science on my side and that was not doing much so what could a book do?* However, when I left her home, I immediately downloaded the book. After listening to it, I began to look at things from a different point of view. I began to look deeper and changed my mindset. *Everything happens for a reason.* My life was about to change because I was going to use all the tools I was learning from reading this book to do so.

What I took from this book was that you are in control of what you want. You speak what you want out into the universe and begin to feel how life would be with whatever it is you are striving for. The universe does the rest. I began to be and feel more positive in life. Yes, from a book and, of course, a good talk with my stepmom. I've listened to this book multiple times and literally learned something new each time. *The Secret* by Rhonda Byrnes has literally changed my life!

Every morning, I started to write in a journal. I would write down all the things I was thankful for. None of my answers from previous days were duplicated. Gratitude was an important point discussed in the book *The Secret*. Showing and feeling gratitude lets the universe know that you are appreciative and ready for the next steps in your destiny. It is so easy to go through life taking things for granted and not taking the time to appreciate who you are as a person, where you are in life, and what you have in life. I was trying to show the universe that I appreciated all I have, my life, my husband, and my marriage. I had to show that I was ready for the next step in my destiny; I was ready for a baby.

My goal was to manifest that child I had longed for. Every morning, I would write baby names in my journal. I spoke about my child as if he were already here and would write, "I am so happy and thankful now that my baby boy is here." I would read this throughout the day and feel as if it were true. You can speak it all day, but you must also feel it in your heart. Like having faith in a way or like adult make-believe. Whatever the case may be, when you begin to manifest your thoughts in a way where you feel like you already have what you are dreaming of, the atmosphere lines up the stars and removes barriers to help you to obtain what it is you are after.

I began to look for baby boy items, as a boy is what I had hoped for. I started to let loose and have fun with the process. I searched for cute maternity clothes, researched what bottles were the best, and even went as far as to look for cute baby Halloween costumes. You get the point! I let my imagination soar to the point where I began to have dreams that mirrored my thoughts.

My mood was brighter, and I honestly began to feel happier. I literally turned a devastating situation into something that was more positive and uplifting to help me and my body to get into a better mood and state for what was to come. I knew it would come because I knew that I was destined for motherhood.

I began to cut out foods that would alter my mood. I didn't consume any artificial sugar as Dr. Kiltz had suggested at our last appointment. He also suggested I increase my protein, so Jesse made me eggs and bacon every morning. My husband and I established an exercise regimen daily in which I would work out for thirty mins to an hour and we began to eat healthy every day. I changed my whole life to build a home for my son that was healthy, strong, and full of all the nutrients and minerals he would need for his nine months in the womb. I guess you can say I was nesting way early in the game.

I continued with the herbal mixture, castor oil packs and acupuncture/massage/cupping. I journaled more, writing down all my thoughts of the day. I started to get rid of toxic people and tried to surround myself with only positivity. I remained positive, and when things got sticky, I would veer myself back on the track of positivity.

I needed my spirit to remain positive, my mindset to remain hopeful, and could not risk negative vibes that could be transferred to me. I did some housekeeping to get into shape mentally, emotionally, spiritually, and physically.

CHAPTER 13

Come On, Baby

I N THE INTERIM, my husband and I continued to try for a baby the old- fashioned way as we contemplated what our next move was. Three months after our last IUI, March 2015, we decided that we were ready to move forward with the IVF. We had been living a healthy lifestyle and we were ready to see if this would help lead us to success.

We were able to get an appointment quite quickly. When we arrived at the appointment, Dr. Kiltz talked about how the IVF process was and what would happen throughout treatment.

I was put on a regimen of medications both orally and injectable. I had never given myself an injection before, but doing so made me feel in control, and again, I was hopeful. I took the meds as prescribed. On April 8, 2015, I gave myself the trigger shot.

The trigger shot is made of the hormone HCG and "triggers" your ovaries to release eggs.

The egg retrieval process was scheduled for April 10, 2015. Egg retrieval carried the possibility of causing pain and cramping, and I needed to avoid cramping like the plague. I again asked to be put under general anesthesia, which Dr. Kiltz agreed to.

Before heading out on retrieval day, Jesse had to provide a semen sample for the fertilization process that we would give the nurse at the clinic. We arrived and were immediately called to the back and again walked to the OR/procedure room to settle in, and I changed into a gown. The nurse asked me questions such as how I felt, and if I had any pain at the time. The anesthesiologist arrived to ask more questions if I had been under anesthesia in the past and if I had any issues with anesthesia with past surgeries; he was simultaneously placing the IV. He informed me I was going to get drowsy, which I do remember, and I guess I passed out shortly after.

When I woke up, my husband was again sitting next to me and the doctor came in shortly after. He explained they obtained nine eggs and would see how many fertilized. I was ecstatic that the medications worked and nine eggs were able to be produced. We were instructed to return to the clinic exactly three days later for embryo transfer. I went home and spent the rest of the day resting and watching movies (as you can see this was one of my favorite past times). I had a bit of cramping, but nothing I was not able to handle.

That weekend after retrieval was my birthday weekend. I made sure I enjoyed myself. I felt the IVF would work, and I celebrated that. My husband took me to dinner, and I was showered with gifts. I planned a get-together at my home in which I had my mother make her famous lasagna. I am surprised I shared this with family and friends. You do not understand how good this shit is; I usually do not share it and instead hide from the world when in the presence of her lasagna! I guess the positivity prompted me to share this time. A few close friends and family members came to the get-together and we jammed to music, danced, and enjoyed each other's company. I felt so elated. The weekend was much needed because before I knew it, the time had come for the embryo transfer.

CHAPTER 14

This Is Really Happening

PRIL 13, 2015, one day before my actual
birthday was embryo transfer day. I was a
little stressed about the procedure, but I was
way more excited. I just knew it in my heart and soul
this IVF would give me a healthy baby.

We arrived early and went straight to the spa and
wellness center to have acupuncture before the procedure, THE PROCEDURE! All our hard work was
going to pay off at this moment.

At the spa, it was the same song and dance for the
acupuncture with a couple of needles in my abdomen
and forehead and a heat lamp over my abdomen. I just
lived in the moment, thinking of all my preparation
for this day. I sunk into my body. Before I knew it, time
was up and the acupuncture treatment was completed.
For the IUIs, the doctor would come to the acupuncture room. This time, we had to walk back to the other

side of the building where the embryo transfer would take place.

It seemed as if the walk to get to that other room took ages, at least it felt that way. The room was quite cozy. There were two doors: one, we used to come in and on the other side, a door where the nurse and doctor would enter. On the left of the exam table was a small screen for the doctor to see where he was placing the embryos. This time, Jesse was required to put on scrubs. We held each other's hands and talked about all the possibilities.

Shortly after, Dr. Kiltz entered the room with the nurse and informed us six eggs matured, but only three fertilized. He asked us how many of the embryos we wanted to transfer and gave us a little time to think it over as he exited the room. I wanted to transfer all three, but my husband and I agreed on two. We informed Dr. Kiltz of our decision as he entered the room. He walked out and returned with a test tube and all the equipment and tools needed for the transfer. He briefly explained the procedure before he began as well as walked us through each step along the way.

I was able to look at the screen placed on the right side of the room to see the embryos being placed. I felt jitters and butterflies as he continued the transfer, my heart full of love and hope and my mind filled with baby shower and nursery ideas. Before I knew it, the transfer was complete and Dr. Kiltz shook our hands and, with a calm and confident voice, said, "We are going to get you that baby." I started to feel what he was saying, *We are going to get that baby!*

Before we left, the nurse gave us a picture of the embryos to keep. These little tiny creatures were just placed in my uterus and could potentially develop into humans. It was so exciting to think about. Science was freaking amazing!!!!

My husband and I walked back across the office for our post acupuncture. Having acupuncture after the embryo transfer increases the chances of embryos implanting in the uterus. Again, the acupuncturist placed the needles on my forehead and abdomen and placed the heat lamp over my abdomen. Jesse and I sat in silence. I think we were both trying to contain our excitement. Before I knew it, time was up, and acupuncture was done.

Before we left, we made an appointment for a fertility massage which I would have that next week. We went home and just spent time together hopeful about the transfer. We were both so scared, excited, and hopeful all wrapped in one.

So, let's talk about pineapples real quick. In all my research, I read that eating the core of the pineapple for five days may help the implantation process. The enzyme in the pineapple, bromelain, is said to increase blood flow to the uterus. Of course, I had to try this; I would try anything to improve chances. Jesse purchased a pineapple and took out the core and I cut it into five pieces so I could consume a piece each day. I thought the pineapple core would be horrible, but it was not as bad as I had thought, hard to chew, but not too bad. I do not know how true the research was, but at that point, I had nothing to lose.

Now, we had to wait and see if all our efforts had actually paid off. The dreaded two week wait.

CHAPTER 15

Best Massage Ever

THOSE NEXT DAYS were a blur as I went to work. The time seemed to go so slowly.

Finally, the day had arrived for me to receive my fertility massage. This is something I had been looking forward to for the whole week. This gave me more hope. Every step I took to help with this journey gave me so much hope. Fertility massage helps with circulation.

This was the most peaceful massage I had thus far. The whole time thinking of this baby that was going to be and all he would bring. I enjoyed every second of this massage and all it had to offer: comfort, nurture, and peace. At the end of the massage, the masseuse placed a cloth on my face with a wonderful smell which I can still not pinpoint, but it was so refreshing and sent endorphins to my brain, boosting my mood.

When she was done, I took my time to get up, as I

wanted the full effects. On my way home, all I thought about was baby shower themes, gender-reveal party ideas, guest lists, nursery, names, and my son's face.

CHAPTER 16

We're Pregnant

APRIL 25TH, 2015, I had to wake up early to get lab work done to check my hCG levels and see if our wish had come true. I felt like my heart was beating out of my chest and my head felt like it was on cloud nine. I kissed my husband as he went to work, and I went to the fertility clinic.

Waiting in the office was so nerve-wracking; I was so over the waiting. Before I knew it, my lab work was taken, and I was told I would find out later that day. Another damn waiting game!

I went to work, and coincidentally, it was my day to work with the GYN specialist; women's health was my passion. The day dragged on until it was finally lunchtime. Jesse came to pick me up for lunch. While we were in the car, I called the doctor to find out the results. As the phone rang and I was put on hold to speak to a nurse, I began to breathe shallow, my heart began to flip, and my palms began to sweat.

As she began to speak the words "your results show… that you are pregnant, congratulations," my body got warm and tingly. We were finally pregnant. *Oh my goodness! Wait, did she just say…? Ahhhhhhhhhhhh!* All the heaviness from my shoulders was lifted. I was calm as I got off the phone and I turned to Jesse and told him the good news. Not only were we excited, but also we were so relieved that we could see the light now that was at the end of the long tunnel we traveled through.

Omg, I had to go back to work after finding out the best news in my life. I could not go back to work after getting the long-awaited news; there was no way I could focus. I informed my preceptor what was going on and asked that I be excused for the day and I am so glad he was agreeable. Jesse drove me back to the office so I could get my car and we headed home. That ride home was crazy.

I could not keep this good news to myself; it was too much. The first person I called was my mother. She was in the car with some other family members on her way to NJ. I spoke low so people she was around could not hear me. "It finally worked, Mom." That was all that I needed to say.

"That is awesome, Taf."

She could not say much, although, later, I found out she wanted to. She did do a Facebook post that day of a picture of her in the car on her way to NJ smiling with the caption: "God is so good, smiling."

The next person I called was my stepmother and father. My stepmother answered the phone and I told her, "Mom, it finally worked."

She was so excited saying, "I told you so."

I waited on the phone with my stepmom as my dad was in the store and I sat on that phone waiting for him to come out. He got on the phone and I said, "Dad, you are going to be a grandpa."

He said, "A what?"

"A grandpa," I repeated.

He sounded so happy and said, "Congratulations, daughter."

"Thank you, Dad. I will keep you both posted."

I had been driving the whole time making calls on my Bluetooth, and before I knew it, we had arrived at our home. The excitement was spilling out of my pores. I needed to go and tell my in-laws.

We got in one car and went to my mother-in-law's house. We played it off by saying that we were just stopping by to say hello. A few minutes into the visit, Jesse said to her, "You will be a grandma soon."

At first, she was so confused and then realized what

Jesse meant and she began smiling with excitement. She immediately picked up the phone to call Papa Nick. I took the phone. Papa Nick was at work, so when he picked up, I said, "Congrats on your promotion."

He said, "What promotion?"

"The promotion of you becoming a grandfather," I replied.

"Oh wow," he said, "I am going to be a grandpa."

I replied, "Yes you are. Now, get back to work and I will talk to you later."

Jesse's mom was still so elated. We spoke for a little while before we ended up leaving to go out to dinner at my favorite place at the time, which was TGI Fridays. I love the sesame jack chicken strips!!! I could not believe this finally happened. I was finally told, "You are pregnant." I felt I was having an out-of-body experience. I never thought I would hear those words. That hole that I had in my heart and soul was finally going to be filled with a bundle of joy. It was my time to be a mother, my husband's time to be a father, and the beginning of our family.

CHAPTER 17

Not Done Yet

THE PROCESS WAS not over quite yet. I had to go to the fertility clinic quite often to get ultrasounds to make sure things were progressing. I remained on the medication regimen, which included some vitamins among other meds, and in addition, I had to have IM progesterone shots every day for the first three months of my pregnancy. Jesse administered these shots every night. With all I put him through during the pregnancy, I am sure he enjoyed giving them. It was because of me we moved twice during the pregnancy and yet Jesse did not complain. He probably held in his frustration and took it out when he injected my ass with progesterone IMs.

I made sure during the process of going back and forth to the fertility clinic that there was someone with me for moral support: my husband or my mother.

My mother was so excited to be having her first

grandchild. She was so loving and supportive, and excited to accompany me to my appointments. Everyone in my support circle was very positive, uplifting and encouraging, and I intended to keep it that way.

CHAPTER 18

Time to Find an OB

THE TIME CAME quickly, too quickly, where I was discharged from Dr. Kiltz and I had the duty of finding an obstetrician. Dr. Kiltz let me know that if I had any questions, he was always there to answer them. He was a major part of that journey, and because of him, his bedside manner, passion, determination, ambition, and skill, he did exactly what he told me he was going to do, which was help us to conceive. Even after being discharged from his care, I would still call him at times to ask questions and he had no issues with answering them. I am forever grateful to have been under the care of Dr. Kiltz.

I received recommendations from friends to a facility that had an awesome reputation for OBGYNs. I called to make an initial appointment. My obstetrician was very nice and down-to-earth. I felt comfortable in his care. Having a great obstetrician we were comfortable with was important to us and we were lucky in finding one.

CHAPTER 19

Getting Prepared

J FACED SO MANY hurdles and knockdowns through-out, but finally got where I needed to be.

Once my son was in the womb, I continued my newfound lifestyle. I remained in a positive state of mind. I continued to write in my journal, and look for maternity clothes and baby items. I tried not to get mad or angry. I stayed surrounded by people who sup-ported and understood what I was going through. All negativity was neglected and ignored. I needed only good feelings going to my baby and no added stress. Although we had to move twice during the pregnancy on account of my pickiness, which did increase stress levels for a short time, my husband made sure that I was comfortable and taken care of emotionally and spiritually. I totally struck gold when I married that man.

I started to take birthing classes. I wanted to be

armed with all the information that was available for the betterment of myself and my child. You can never be overprepared because a parenting manual doesn't exist.

CHAPTER 20

A Great Pregnancy

M Y NINE MONTHS of pregnancy was awesome. I often still, to this day, tell people this, and nine out of ten times, I get the crazy look. That is the truth. I absolutely loved being pregnant. Every aspect of it. It meant everything to me to experience the pregnancy and everything it came with.

My first trimester, my appetite was off. I would get nauseous often and stick to things such as rice and fruit. I used to love orange juice in the morning, but during pregnancy, I couldn't stand the smell. Meat, any kind, would aggravate the symptoms. Jesse loves chicken and burgers, so those were always cooking and just the raw smell of it was something I could not tolerate. To this day, I cut down on my meat intake and I would not call myself a vegetarian, but close to it, and orange juice has been forever eliminated from my diet.

In my second trimester, we found out the sex of

the baby. My husband, my cousin Fysha, and I went to the doctors together for the appointment. Our plan was to have a gender-reveal party at my favorite place, TGI Fridays; seriously, the sesame jack chicken, heaven on earth! When the ultrasound technician asked if we wanted to know, how could any of us resist? Jesse expressed he wanted to be the first to know and did not want to find out with everyone else anyways. My husband, such a rebel. The technician informed us that it was indeed a boy! We were all elated. We planned to keep it a secret and would all act surprised at the gender-reveal party.

On the day of the party, we would reveal by pulling a boy's outfit out of a gift bag to show everyone. Jesse and I headed to the baby store to purchase an outfit for the big reveal.

We had about three-quarters of the family who wanted us to have a boy and one quarter who wanted us to have a girl. Those who were team-girl wore pink and those who were team-boy wore red (no blue, Jesse didn't like blue).

We waited for our appetizers before I stood up and pulled the outfit out of the bag we had chosen. The look on my face was priceless. I was such a good actor and did not give up the info I had already known a week prior. Someone captured a picture of that look on my face and it is forever on the internet.

A couple of weeks later, I was able to feel my little

man move. This first happened at work when I was sitting at my desk. They do not prepare you for exactly how it feels when this first happens. I kid you not; at first, I thought I had gas and did not think twice about it. When it happened again later that day, I was like, *Oh, wait, is this the baby moving?* Damn right, my little man was in there and was making his presence known. I loved that feeling of him moving all around in my belly. I remember my little cousin Talitha was over at my house and I asked her to feel the baby move, and when she did, she could feel all his little bones which freaked her right out. You should have seen the expression on her face.

For the longest time, Jesse was not able to feel the baby move. I am not sure if this was just the baby being stubborn or what. For weeks, Jesse would feel, and baby boy was not making much movement. Finally, lying in bed watching television with his hand on my belly, he was able to feel the baby finally move. It was so exciting to have him feel the same thing I was feeling. This was so special for both of us.

Let's talk about hemorrhoids! So, no one prepares you for *e v e r y t h i n g*. I developed a huge hemorrhoid that caused so much pain for weeks, and for weeks, I could not sleep or was awakened by the pain from it. The pain would shoot down my legs and cause numbness, and at times, weakness.

After weeks of dealing with this grape-sized

appendage, it finally shrunk down and went away. What a hell of a time those couple of weeks were. Even so, I still enjoyed being pregnant. That was part of my pregnancy journey and I was just happy to be at that stage.

The heartburn was a killer. It would wake me up in the middle of the night or impact my sleep. I continued to deal with it right up until the end. I've heard people mention how bad it could be and thought they were over-exaggerating, but as I went through it, I knew they weren't. That constant burning sensation in your chest and "globus sensation" in your throat was very much uncomfortable, but I managed, TUMS seemed to help with some relief!

The third trimester is when we decided to have our baby shower. My mother and mother-in-law rented the venue and my stepmom and dad hired a coordinator. This was a major deal because our son was everyone's first (son, grandson, great-grandson, and nephew). We had to celebrate in style. Everyone made a Thanksgiving-themed dish and we had mini apple and pumpkin pies as favors. The overall theme of the baby shower was music, as both Jesse and I are avid fans. My grandfather and Aunt Angie traveled from Philadelphia to be there for that day. This little boy would indeed be spoiled.

The games were awesome, the vibes were great, and the gifts were astronomical. It was such a blessing to have all my friends and family come out to celebrate with us. This moment was memorable for Jesse and me.

It was in my third trimester I started to have difficulty getting comfortable. All I kept hearing in my head was "lie on your left side," "make sure you sleep on your left side," "don't forget to rest on your left side." I felt like a prisoner because I am one who tosses and turns a lot. I ended up giving in and purchasing the pregnancy pillow. This was the greatest investment ever. Thank you, pregnancy pillow Gods. This helped with insomnia and I was finally able to get a restful, comfortable sleep when the heartburn didn't keep me up.

CHAPTER 21

Induction

I N MY THIRD trimester, I was instructed to go to the doctor weekly for an NST.

NST (non-stress test) is a screening tool used in pregnancy to evaluate the fetal heart rate and responsiveness.

Again, I made sure to go with either my husband or mother for moral support. My grandmother even went a few times.

This was ordered because as the pregnancy progressed, my blood pressure increased. I did not mind going because it was so relaxing, and I got to hear and see the heartbeat every time.

At thirty-nine weeks, I went to my regularly scheduled appointment, and after taking my blood pressure, the doctor said, "You need to go for induction, your blood pressure is too high."

My husband and I stopped home to get ours and the baby's bag. The time was finally here where we were going to meet our son. Although I had nested early on, I had to make sure everything would be perfect when our baby came home. I did some light tidying up, and when I was done, we headed to the hospital. We went to security, checked in, and headed for the fourth floor, maternity.

When we arrived on the maternity unit, we had to check in again, and shortly after, we were assigned a room. It was all so surreal. I can remember doing clinical on this floor during nursing school and seeing other mothers as they labored and anticipated the day when it would be me. When they put the monitor on my belly, it made it that much more surreal. We settled in before giving the nurse my birth plan I drafted up. We texted and called everyone we needed to and informed them of the news that the baby would be coming soon. Little did we know how long we would have to wait for this little bugger to arrive.

To get the induction process, the doctor started with cervidil.

Cervidil is a vaginal suppository used to relax and soften the cervix.

After twelve hours, the doctor came to check if I had dilated, and I had, but only two centimeters. So they decided to place another cervidil. When they checked twelve hours later, I only dilated to five centimeters. Day number two of being on the labor and delivery floor and one more time with the cervidil. This time, when the doctor checked after twelve hours, there was no progression. Stuck at five centimeters.

The doctor moved on to balloon dilation. A catheter with a balloon at the end was inserted into my cervix and the doctor inflated with saline solution. This method helps by putting pressure on the cervix to encourage dilation. When this was initially inserted, it caused so much pain; I wanted it taken out. As he deflated the balloon a little, it was more tolerable. I agreed to the balloon dilation but only if it was not inflated fully and the doctor was agreeable to my request. A few hours later, the doctor returned to check my progression and I was at six centimeters. *Ok, Tyson, so are you purposely not trying to vacate the premises?*

The doctor decided, at that time, he should break my water to help the process along. I had heard horror stories from other mothers when their waters were broken. I hesitated but knew it was necessary. Quick and fast and then the bed was full of fluid and it was not painful at all. He came back to check a few hours later, and still, no progression, still stuck at six centimeters. *Ok, Tyson, for real, cut the crap!*

This whole time, I was having contractions, but because I was so happy to have gotten to be able to conceive, I did not take the pain the same way. In a way, I enjoyed the pain. I enjoyed the process of being pregnant, laboring. My in-laws even came up for a few hours and we watched *Family Guy* and *American Dad* reruns! The laughter helped to keep my mind off the pain. Everyone was anticipating this little dude and he was not ready to make an appearance.

I had not slept, as the contractions were all over the place and most of the pain was in my lower back. I used the hot tub on the maternity floor a couple of times for relief and tried different positions on the bed for comfort. Thank goodness we purchased some massage devices and Jesse continued to use those throughout the contractions to help relieve the pain in my back.

After no progression with the water breaking, the doctor decided to give Pitocin. *Great, another intervention that I heard horror stories about.* However, I knew it wouldn't be that bad. Everything people told me about labor was bullshit, but then again that was their story they were telling, and I was creating my own. The nurse came in, hooked my IV up to the medication, and started to run the Pitocin. The contractions started to come more frequently and got a little more painful but nothing that I could not handle. This was run for a while, and when the doctor returned, I still had not progressed.

Although I had put in my birth plan I wanted a natural birth, the providers felt that it would be in my best interest to have an epidural to help ease some of the pain. I was hesitant at first, as this was not my plan and I wanted to feel e v e r y t h i n g. There was a very compassionate resident on the floor who sort of read my mind, and without me initiating the conversation, she stated, "Just because you get meds does not make you any less of a mother."

It is so funny how things work. She could see I was in pain as I continued to try multiple remedies for comfort and relief among trying many other interventions to help with induction. We were on day three and I still had not progressed, and the contractions continued; with the Pitocin, they were stronger. I agreed with the resident; it was time for an epidural. When the staff came to place the epidural, it was not as bad as I had imagined. It was a quick procedure and the pain started to ease quickly as my legs literally went numb and I could not move much anymore. My husband had to shift me due to my legs having no sensation.

A few hours later, doctors and nurses ran in stating that the baby's heart rate dropped. They needed to do an emergency C-section. *Finally, I would meet this little guy that was being stubborn.* He had to come out now. I was so tired at this point but excited; finally, this would be it and he would be in my arms.

It was not long before we were in the OR with Jesse on my right side. Before they started, I was so scared; I said to the doctors, "How do you know that I am **numb numb**?"

He replied with a chuckle, "We did a trial cut and you did not feel it."

I chuckled in relief. They informed me that I would feel a lot of pulling, tugging, and pressure. That is just what I felt, so much pushing and pulling and tugging, and then a big pull, and then a cry. *Wait, really, that is it, that quick?* As our baby boy cried, I looked at my husband with mist in my eyes. The nurse came over to show me my son and then took him to clean him off and check him. Jesse went over to hold him. The nurse finally passed my beautiful baby boy to me and I could not wait to have skin to skin contact for the first time. This was unbelievable to me. I felt all emotions at once running through my veins. December 30, 2015, a miracle baby was born.

We were pushed to recovery and were only supposed to be there for thirty mins. Turns out that, of course, my blood pressure would not stabilize, and we were there for about five hours. The staff was so great and knew we had family waiting and allowed them to come into the recovery room to see us two at a time. I was so amazed at everyone who came out to see Tyson, and everyone who saw his beautiful face was in awe of him. Everyone got a little emotional because Tyson was the first for everyone.

Shortly after the visits, my blood pressure stabilized, and we were transported to the postpartum unit. It was about one o'clock in the morning at this time. My mother and Aunt Nana purchased me a sub from Wegmans prior to coming to see Tyson. This was my favorite and I could not eat cold cuts during pregnancy. The sub had everything on it (I usually do not get subs with the works, but by this time I did not even care because that was something I had craved for months) and I devoured it at one o'clock in the morning. *Yaassssssss Wegmans!*

We were in the hospital for New Year's Eve and I remember watching the specials. *What a way to bring in the New Year with a new baby.* New Year's Day, the doctor allowed us to go home. Makes a total of five days we were in the hospital. All worth every second. Now, the real journey was to begin.

CHAPTER 22
Back with a Vengeance

T HROUGHOUT MY PREGNANCY right up until my son was thirteen months old, I did not have many, if any, endometriosis symptoms. I breastfed for thirteen months, not only for the good of my son but also to avoid my period. As soon as the first period made an appearance, I got the symptoms I had prior to my pregnancy in addition to new symptoms I had never experienced.

To add to the excruciating pelvic pain I had with my period, I now experienced constant pelvic pain at varying degrees of intensity, back pain, fatigue, and nausea. Additionally, lightheadedness, dizziness, vomiting, diarrhea, pain with urination, extreme hot flashes, severe rectal pain, longer menstrual cycles, and severe right shoulder pain.

The shoulder pain was the first new symptom I noticed. At first, I thought maybe my bra strap was too tight or I slept the wrong way. Every month, it was the same thing, two to three days before my period. It took me a bit to realize this was a pattern. It was so weird, but a great predictor of when my period was coming. This pain lasted the whole length of my period but lessened towards the end.

Rectal pain would start as soon as my period began. Felt like I had a raging hemorrhoid every month. I could not sit normally at work or at home. I would sit to the side, sort of on my hip when I was at work. If I sat normally, the pain would be too intense to bear. At home, I would sit on heat to help ease the pain, but the pain was deeper than the heat could reach, and most of the time, it did not help.

Before having Tyson, the length of the period was four to five days when I used the birth control and lengthened once I stopped. After Tyson, the length of periods went from seven days to two weeks. Yes, two weeks of fatigue, bleeding and feeling drained and useless. I never knew how it felt to want to rip out your uterus until I started to have these two-week periods. Really, two weeks? Who thought that was a good idea?

The fatigue I experienced with my periods was unbearable. I was not able to do much the first four to five days except lie down. I found myself not being able to work at times for a few days. I could literally nap anywhere when the fatigue set in and my favorite part of the day was bedtime.

I have heard of how hot flashes feel and I always thought people would exaggerate it. I am here to say NO ONE IS EXXAGERATING! Who in the world thought women should go through bleeding monthly and then on top of that walk through hell for a few minutes? Your whole entire body feels as if it is heated, but from the inside, and you can't cool down, no matter what you do. Thank goodness it only lasts a few minutes, but geez what a gift to women. I would often ask Jesse, "Why do you have the heat on?"

He would reply, "Babe, I do not think that is the heat."

I laugh about it now and I know I drove him crazy.

The lightheadedness and dizziness kicked in around the same time, which was day one or two of my period and the hot flashes came with them. These symptoms would present when I was either getting dressed or in the bathroom. I would feel the dizziness, then the hot flash, and then the lightheadedness. When the symptoms appeared, I always had to lower myself to the floor because I always would feel as if I was going to fall or faint. I would crawl to the stair to yell for my husband or to my phone to text him to come and help me. Minutes later, every time, nausea started. With nausea came vomiting and/or dry heaves.

The pelvic pain went from only presenting during my period to all the time, which was accompanied by back pain. This was worst a few days before my period and then throughout. Throughout the month, the pain remained to some degree. The worst was after orgasms. The pelvic pain lasted one to two days after orgasm and I felt as if my pelvis was burning or on fire. *Wonderful!*

Ok, endometriosis, I see you got some type of point to make!

CHAPTER 23

Let's Play a Game

NOW, I HAD a toddler to keep up with, a husband to take care of, and a house to keep. I went to the doctor pleading for help. He put me back on birth control pills to help suppress the symptoms. These pills did absolutely nothing. They did, however, decrease the length of the period. This was the birth control roulette game all over again. *Is this déjà vu?*

Dealing with the pain and other symptoms caused me to go back into the dark hole. The pain was intolerable both physically and mentally. I would often cry to myself at night because nothing was helping. I tried to keep the depression to myself as not to burden my family with this again. It was getting more out of hand than before. I, again, did not want to get out of bed. I only wanted to sleep. I began to isolate myself in the house and avoid social activities. I thought of death a lot. How the pain would be gone if I were to. These thoughts increased my depression more. I knew that I needed to get my shit together. I had a family and needed to be strong for them as well as myself. I had goals in life and was not close to accomplishing them all. Something had to give!

After feeling down and beginning this cycle again, I knew that was not the road I wanted to walk. I began to read books on positivity again, write in my journal and was directed back to my positive lifestyle. My insight increased when I was veering off track. I had tools that I was learning and had learned that I would use to help place me back on track.

I knew the pills did not work in the past and again was not doing much. I did remember the NuvaRing had helped in the past. I figured I'd like to try NuvaRing again, but because of my high blood pressure, the doctor would not prescribe it. I went for a second opinion and this provider was agreeable with my request. *Thank goodness.*

As expected, my blood pressure spiked back up and I was put back on medications, but I would have rather taken a pill to help lower my blood pressure vs dealing with the endometriosis and its associated symptoms without an effective method of relief.

CHAPTER 24

Be Your Own Advocate

THIS IS YOUR life, so you must speak up and be the boss of it. You must advocate for yourself!

1. The first piece of advice I would give is to always keep a log. Whatever it is you are going to be seen for, make sure you have notes. Write down when the symptoms started, what the symptoms are, how long the symptoms have been present for, whether or not the symptoms are constant or more prevalent at different times of the day, things you have tried to help decrease the symptoms, and aggravating factors or things that make the symptoms worse. This not only helps you but also helps your provider get the whole story to be able to better diagnose and treat you.

2. Bring a notebook to the office to keep notes throughout the appointment. You may want to go back and look at things you would like to research further or things you forgot that were mentioned during the appointment. This notebook will serve as a reference for you, your doctor, and any specialty doctor that you see. Write down all the vital information your provider tells you including diagnoses, tests, or procedures that are necessary, specialists you may need to go see, medications suggested and/or recommended, and dosing and frequency of that medication(s).

3. Always have someone with you. This second person should be someone you trust. They will be there to be your second set of ears and ask questions that maybe you wouldn't have thought to ask.

4. Always have your phone on vibrate and away unless you have notes on your phone. Turning your phone down will decrease distraction. The time you have with your provider in your appointment is limited and you want to make sure you are treating it as such. In addition, you will appreciate not getting distracted when asking questions, taking notes, or when

the provider is explaining important information to you.

5. ASK ASK ASK!! Do not be afraid to be that patient that asks questions. No question is stupid, and you should not feel ashamed, rushed, or scared to ask anything. This is your life and your health, and you have the right to ask questions so you can better understand. It is important you and the provider work together as a team to better your health. If you are feeling rushed or feel as though the provider is not listening to you or not answering your questions, address this with your provider. If actions are not changed to accommodate your request, then you have the right to find another provider who you feel more comfortable with. Make sure you and your provider are on the same page and are working together collaboratively.

6. If you feel you want to research your health condition, diagnostic test, or medication, I would encourage you to do so; however, use a reputable source.

Advocate for yourself and be serious about doing so. Again, this is your life and your health. Who else is going to look out for it if you don't?

CHAPTER 25

Changing Your Mindset

MANY PEOPLE WOULD say that having endometriosis, depression, and issues with fertility is unlucky or a curse. I see it as a windfall. Walking this path has helped me become better in tune with my body mentally, emotionally, and spiritually. I began to reflect on who I was, where I was, and where I was going vs where I wanted to go. I was more vigilant with what I fed myself mentally, emotionally and spiritually. Negative thoughts would try to cloud my mind and take over, but I learned to combat them using many different tools I learned on the way. I had to pay attention to what and whom I allowed in my space so that I would not get thrown off balance by any negative vibes.

Replacing negative thoughts with positive thoughts is a great tool to learn. When I began to have a negative thought, I would acknowledge it, and then replace it with something positive. For instance, instead of asking "why me?" I would ask "what is the universe trying to teach me?" I stopped entertaining those negative thoughts and letting them marinate in my head because all that did was give them life and cause more negative thoughts to transpire. You attract what you think, and my goal was only to attract positive. It takes practice, but it is worth the time and effort.

I began to use daily affirmations to boost my confidence and mood. It was a daily pep talk I would give myself every morning to set the tone for that day. It not only made me feel good but also it empowered me and made me feel unstoppable as if anything that was thrown at me I could handle with ease.

I continued my daily journaling of the things I was grateful for and why I was grateful for them. I practiced gratitude every day so the universe knew I was ready for the next road, and for the next phase of my destiny. You can't expect the universe to give you a promotion if you aren't giving 1000 percent in your current role. Think about it this way, there was a time that you prayed to be where you are right now; be grateful and rejoice in knowing the stars were aligned for you to make it there.

I stopped taking things for granted. I was an otherwise healthy twenty-seven-year-old, but could not conceive a child with my husband naturally. My goal was not going according to plan. This was part of my problem. I had goals mapped out and I had ages I wanted to accomplish those goals I strived for. Conceiving was not something I had much control over, and it bothered me to know that. I had to let go and let the universe work its magic. The universe was teaching me I could not be in control of every aspect. I had to learn this before I could grow. I had to understand that what is meant to be will be, and when the time is right, the universe would inform me of this.

After changing my mindset, I understood and believed that there were a few reasons trying to conceive was not happening at the time I wanted it to. I needed to be stronger mentally. There is a reason for everything. What I mean by this is that I now see things differently. If it were not for me going through this, I wouldn't have grown through it. I would have probably never discovered I needed to grow in order to manifest my destiny. I wouldn't have recognized that I needed to change my surroundings and mentality to only reflect positivity. I wouldn't have changed my diet much to create a healthy home for my son. I wouldn't have been as physically active as I was prior to having my son. Everything really does start in your head and I am so grateful I learned that.

This experience mentally prepared me for motherhood. No one is ever ready for motherhood because no one knows what to expect. I felt I could take whatever it was that motherhood would throw at me because my mindset had changed. There was no way I would be able to control everything when my child was born and I had to accept that. Parenting is not easy by any means but I was more prepared because of my change in mindset.

I strongly believe I was given this path to walk to be comfortable enough to want to share my story with other women who may be suffering through the same trials and tribulations. Prior to this experience, I did not have anyone I knew that had the same or similar experience(s). I did not feel as though I could relate to many in my family or friends with this topic, which is why I kept it mostly to myself until recently. Now, I want to be the woman other women can call on or relate to if they are going through this or similar experience.

I can finally say I am not ashamed anymore and I am not going to let endometriosis, infertility, or depression have a hold on me to the point of embarrassment, or disrupt my peace of mind. Besides, I grew through those experiences and I am continuing to. They do not define me, but they helped me to define who I am and want to be.

Glossary

Adhesion is scar tissue that binds together and acts as a binding agent, causing organs to stick together. Adhesions normally form after surgery.

Cervidil is a vaginal suppository used to relax and soften the cervix.

Dysmenorrhea means painful periods.

EMLA is an anesthetic that is used to numb the skin prior to a medical procedure.

Endometriosis is a painful disorder in which endometrial-like tissue (tissue that resembles the lining that normally covers the inside of the uterus) grows outside of the uterus on organs. The endometrial growths bleed monthly mimicking the menses. Besides pain, it can cause gastrointestinal issues, and binding of your organs as well as many other varying symptoms.

Exploratory laparoscopic surgery is a minimally invasive surgery in which the surgeon places tiny incisions in your abdominal wall to look at the abdominal and reproductive organs to help diagnose certain diseases.

Fertility acupuncture is said to help by decreasing stress. Acupuncture also increases blood flow to the reproductive systems. With this process, the endocrine system is also balanced.

HCG (human chorionic gonadotropin) is a hormone that is produced during pregnancy after implantation takes place.

HSG (hysterosalpingogram) is a test in which a dye is placed through the cervix and x-rays are then taken to evaluate. The test helps to determine if the tubes are blocked as well as help determine the shape of the uterus.

Hydrosalpinx is a blocked fallopian tube filled with fluid.

Irritable bowel syndrome is an intestinal disorder causing symptoms such as abdominal pain, nausea, vomiting, diarrhea, and constipation.

IUI is intrauterine insemination in which the sperm is placed in the uterus to facilitate fertilization.

IVF (in vitro fertilization) is a combination of meds and medical procedure which helps the sperm to fertilize an egg. The eggs are retrieved from the woman after helping to get to an optimal state. Once they are retrieved, the egg(s) and sperm are manually combined in a dish. Once fertilization takes place, then the egg(s) are placed back in the uterus.

The lysis of adhesions is a procedure in which scar tissue that causes chronic pelvic and abdominal pain is destroyed.

NST (non-stress test) is a screening tool used in pregnancy to evaluate the fetal heart rate and responsiveness.

An ovarian cyst is a solid or fluid-filled sac within or on the surface of the ovary.

Stage 4 endometriosis is the "severe" stage where deep endometriosis implants, cysts, and adhesions invade your organs.

The trigger shot is made of the hormone HCG and it "triggers" your ovaries to release eggs.

Upper GI series is an x-ray exam of your upper GI tract that is made visible by drinking a liquid solution.

Epilogue

SEVENTEEN YEARS LATER, and I still struggle with the daily pelvic pain, pain after orgasms, spells of nausea, dizziness and lightheadedness, bowel habit changes, and varying degrees of fatigue. I have been trying different eating habits, herbals, and supplements, but have not identified the precise combination quite yet. I am still learning the best way to cope with these symptoms, but I am not giving up. I fight through to keep myself on track. I am refusing to let endometriosis have a hold on my life. I have too much to live for and so much I still have to do.

The depression tries to peek in every once in a while. I still have times when I get into a hole where it takes more effort to pull myself out of, but I remember what I've learned and how far I have come and I am able to dig myself out of it quicker than in the past. I can't allow myself to go down the dark hole where this condition has taken me in the past, twice before. This part of the journey is a work in progress.

I continue with my affirmations, positive thoughts, and expressions of my gratitude.

My affirmations change depending on where I am in my life and what my goal is, but I continue that pep talks to myself. It gets me pumped like a coach talking to his players before a game. Only, in this scenario, I am the player and the coach, and because of that, I work twice as hard.

I have become better at replacing my negative thoughts with positive ones. I still continue to acknowledge the negative thoughts, but as I said before, I do not entertain them. I replace that thought with a positive to help me stay on track with this journey of positivity.

When I get up every morning and before I go to bed every night, I think about all the things I am grateful for, big and small. I acknowledge I have come a long way and, although I'm still trying to get where I want to be, I made it this far, which I am truly grateful for.

I am not perfect by any means and that is not my goal. My goal is to be better than I was yesterday, continue to learn, and grow into someone that my son will look up to and someone I am proud to be.

Seventeen years after this whole ordeal began, and here I am still standing strong, growing, learning, and advocating for other women.

If you would have asked me seventeen years ago, I would have never thought I would be speaking about any of this. I never felt as if I had a voice, and when I realized I did, I gained momentum. Now, I continue to speak my truth to anyone who will listen.

This condition has literally taken me to hell and I was able to climb out of the fire and turn that situation into my story. My story to share with girls and women going through the same or similar situations. I refused to stay in a state of damnation.

It took me time, but I am here. From this journey, I have gained direction to go down a new path. I have gained more knowledge about the condition. I have become a better mother, woman, and human. I appreciate and am grateful for my journey because if it were not for that, I would not have grown, learned, or gained a voice in the matter.

We are all put on this earth for a purpose and my purpose is this!

My goal is to continue to raise awareness for this condition so young girls can have a better chance at earlier treatment in an attempt to decrease some of the long-term effects that can arise like infertility.

I will continue to use my voice to make the difference and I am confident that my voice will be the difference!

Acknowledgments

To my mother, thank you so much for being there for me when I felt so alone and broken. It meant a lot when you made it your duty to be at some of the doctor's appointments with me to make sure I was not alone. You accompanied me to some of the birthing classes that were held in the evening hours and did not complain about being there with me and for me. Even when I was admitted for induction, you stayed at the hospital with me and Jesse until Tyson was born. You slept on a cot in the hospital room next to me for three days and did not complain about it. You are awesome and I truly appreciate that you were there for me. You were very encouraging throughout the process and it put me more at ease to know you were there for me through it all.

To my stepmother, Tafara, thank you so much for being the word of reason for me when I was starting to lose all hope. I will always remember those words we exchanged when I came to you depressed about not being able to conceive. It is because of you, your words of advice, and your book suggestion that I have continued to grow as a woman. I never knew a book could do so much. I do not think I would have even given it a second thought if you had not expressed to me how it helped you in your life. You give THE BEST advice and I am so glad to be able to call you my step-mother. You definitely are a great one and I appreciate having you in my life.

To MY AUNT NANA, you did not know I was going through struggles with fertility or depression, but you sensed something wrong as you always do. I appreciate how you know me so well to be able to know when I am not myself. You took time and just hugged me for what felt like forever. You gave me words of encouragement without even knowing the situation. Your hugs leave a major impression! Best hugs ever by far! Thank you, Nana!

To MY BIG BROTHER DAVID HICKS (D. L. HICKS), I want to thank you for all the pointers, for listening to my story and encouraging me to keep going. Thanks for helping me to come up with phrases for my book to make it even better. I appreciate you so much and I'm glad we are as close as we are. Love you, big bro!

To MY COUSIN TEONNA, you are truly an inspiration. You have done so much for me to help me on my writing journey. You listen to my ideas, give me feedback, and helped to lead me down a path of success. You have given me the opportunity to co-blog on your website for more exposure and I cannot express how much that means. I am so glad we are beginning to build our relationship because you are very special, my love. Love you, cuzzo!

To Dr. Kiltz, you truly are the best at what you do. I appreciate your compassion, determination, care, and love you show to your patents. You told me from the start that no matter what it took, you were going to make sure my husband and I got our baby. What more can I say; you stuck by your word and by our side as we struggled with this obstacle in our lives. You made yourself available whenever we needed you and answered all and any questions we had throughout the process. We greatly appreciate you and all you do. Thank you so much! You have become part of our story and, as far as I am concerned, part of our family! Keep being great!!!

To Annette, you truly are a special person. I did not know what to expect when I started treatment with you. Your knowledge and compassion easily put my mind right at ease. I trusted everything you told me and everything you did. I would be so excited to have my weekly appointments with you because I knew you were healing me and my body. I appreciate you so much for being there at my worst and helping me to get to my best! Thank you for all you have done for me.

About the Author

Writer, blogger, educator, family nurse practitioner, and author of *Grow Through It*.

Tafiea remains the President of Team Syracuse Worldwide EndoMarch raising awareness for endometriosis.

Tafiea has a background in mental health and worked in the field for three years as an RN. As a nurse practitioner, she has worked in primary care and adult medicine. She is passionate about women's health and takes every opportunity with her female patients to ask necessary questions about common women's health issues, especially if endometriosis is suspected.

Tafiea lives in Syracuse, NY with her toddler son, Tyson and loving husband, Jesse.

Facebook:
Tafiea Stokes
Instagram:
@Tafiea_stokes
Website:
www.tafieastokes.com
Email:
Tafiea.stokes@gmail.com

Letter to the Reader

Thank you for taking the time to read about and understand my journey.

I hope that in reading *Grow Through It,* you are able
to use some of the information to help you in your
own lives.

From reading my story, I hope it evoked some
inspiration for you to be able to begin to speak up and
out about your story. Even if you aren't ready to speak
yet, I hope this book is the starting point for you to
start that process.

Remember, it is up to you to improve the scenery on your path and it all starts with your thoughts.
Your thoughts determine your actions, so change your
mindset to change your path.

Signed,

Tafiea Stokes

Made in the USA
Lexington, KY
17 November 2019

57182489R00074